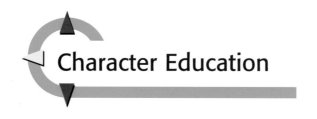

Character Education

Loyalty

by Lucia Raatma

Consultant:
Madonna Murphy, Ph.D.
Professor of Education
University of St. Francis, Joliet, Illinois
Author, *Character Education in America's
Blue Ribbon Schools*

Bridgestone Books
an imprint of Capstone Press
Mankato, Minnesota

Bridgestone Books are published by Capstone Press
151 Good Counsel Drive, P.O. Box 669, Mankato, Minnesota 56002
http://www.capstone-press.com

Library of Congress Cataloging-in-Publication Data
Raatma, Lucia.
    Loyalty / by Lucia Raatma.
    p. cm.—(Character education)
    Summary: Explains the virtue of loyalty and describes ways to show it in the home,
school, and community.
    Includes bibliographical references and index.
    ISBN 0-7368-1390-X (hardcover)
    1. Loyalty—Juvenile literature. [1. Loyalty.] I. Title. II. Series.
BJ1533.L8 R32 2003
179'.9—dc21   2001007905

Editorial Credits

Megan Schoeneberger, editor; Karen Risch, product planning editor; Steve Christensen,
    series designer; Heidi Meyer, book designer and illustrator; Alta Schaffer, photo researcher;
    Nancy White, photo stylist

Photo Credits

Capstone Press/Jim Foell, 6, 8, 10, 16, 20
Corbis/Bettmann, 18
Corbis Stock Market/Tim & Dee Ann McCarthy, 12
Corbis/Tim Wright, cover
Jim Baron/The Image Finders, 14
Skjold Photographs, 4

1 2 3 4 5 6 07 06 05 04 03 02

Table of Contents

Loyalty

Loyalty is about being faithful to your family, friends, and to your beliefs. Loyalty also means loving your country. Loyal people sometimes have to stand up for their beliefs. A loyal person builds strong bonds with family and friends.

faithful
steady and worthy of trust

Being Loyal

Loyalty means keeping commitments. Maybe you want to join a club. Be loyal and attend your club's meetings. You also may have promised to be a good friend. You can be loyal to people who matter to you.

commitment
a promise to do something

Loyalty at Home

Being loyal to your family members keeps your family strong. Maybe a parent lost a job. Comfort your parent. Be loyal to your parent and support her while she looks for a new job. You are loyal when you support your family no matter what.

Loyalty with Your Friends

Loyal friends keep each other's secrets. They stick up for their friends if others are teasing them. Loyal people spend time with their friends. You are loyal when you listen to friends who are sad or upset.

Loyalty at School

Being loyal to your school shows you care about it. You can wear your school's colors and learn your school's song. You are loyal when you cheer for your school's teams. A loyal person supports these teams whether they win or lose.

Loyalty in Sports

Loyalty is an important part of teamwork. Being loyal means supporting your teammates even if they make mistakes. You are loyal when you play your best.

Loyalty in Your Community

Loyalty means caring for your community and your country. You can obey police officers and fire fighters. Be proud of your country. Show your loyalty by saying the Pledge of Allegiance. Loyal people keep communities strong.

Pledge of Allegiance
a promise to be loyal
to the United States

17

"Look at these grand men. Which one of you wouldn't consider it the highlight of his career just to associate with them for even one day?"

—Lou Gehrig, talking to his fans about his Yankee teammates

Loyal Lou Gehrig

Lou Gehrig played baseball for the New York Yankees from 1923 to 1939. Lou was loyal to both his fans and his teammates. He chose to stay with the Yankees for his whole career. He played 2,130 games in a row. This number was a record for many years.

career
the work or the jobs that a person has

Loyalty and You

You must make choices when you are loyal. You choose what is important in your life. You choose to stand up for your beliefs. Being loyal is not always easy. But people trust you when you are loyal. People will be loyal to you in return.

Hands On: Make a Family Tree

Learning about your family can help you be loyal. You can learn about your family by making a family tree.

What You Need

An older family member
Large sheet of paper
Markers or crayons

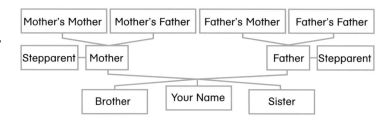

What You Do

1. Talk to an older family member. Ask for the full names of your grandparents and parents. Listen to stories about your family.
2. Look at the example above. Draw four boxes across the top of the paper. Write your grandparents' names inside the boxes.
3. Follow the example above to add two more boxes. List your parents' names in these two boxes.
4. Add another box below your parents' boxes. List your name in this box.
5. Add boxes for brothers, sisters, or stepparents. List their names in the boxes.

Look at your family tree. See how everyone in your family is connected. Being loyal to your family will make these bonds even stronger.

Words to Know

bond (BOND)—a close friendship with someone

cheer (CHIHR)—to shout encouragement; loyal people cheer for their teams to win and also support their teams when they lose.

faithful (FAYTH-fuhl)—steady and worthy of trust; being faithful means loving and supporting your friends and family no matter what.

support (suh-PORT)—to help and encourage someone

Read More

Adler, David A. *Lou Gehrig: The Luckiest Man.* San Diego: Harcourt Brace, 1997.

Brown, Laurene Krasny, and Marc Brown. *How to Be a Friend: A Guide to Making Friends and Keeping Them.* Boston: Little, Brown, 1998.

Internet Sites

Adventures from the Book of Virtues
http://www.pbs.org/adventures
Crossroads of Character
http://library.thinkquest.org/J001675F/?tqskip=1
Lou Gehrig Official Site
http://www.lougehrig.com

Index